Mark my words

Insights and observations on life... and how to live it well

C000150514

MARK O'NEILL

2QT Limited (Publishing)

2QT Limited (Publishing)
Settle
North Yorkshire
BD24 9RH
United Kingdom

Cover and internal graphics: Hilary Pitt
Images: Shutterstock.com

Printed in Great Britain by Lightning Source UK

A CIP catalogue record for this book is available
from the British Library
ISBN 978-1-912014-70-5

For my son

Dearest Anne-Marie,

For the next chapter —
may it be everything you
wish for.
All my love,
Claire
xxo —

1

If you are wondering whether to offer a handshake

...offer a handshake

2

Never let fear of confrontation stop you
doing the right thing

3

Sometimes people are just plain wrong
– be prepared for this

4

Your heart tells you what you want;
your head tells you what other people say you
should want

5

It is better to fight and lose than not to fight at all

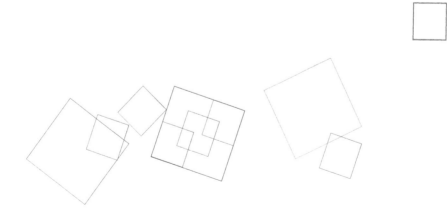

6

When someone says 'I hear what you are saying' they really mean 'I don't like what you are saying'

7

Learn how to
put up a shelf

8

Recognise what you like
and don't like

Self discipline is the key to success

10

Do press-ups

Keep up one form of exercise to stay fit –
either the one you enjoy most or one that is practical

12

Be busy but not over-busy; allow time to enjoy life

13

Be ruthless about cutting things out of your life that you haven't got time, or space, for

14

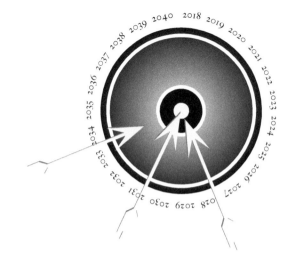

Make a list of goals every New Year

15

'There's no such thing as a joke'

16

When learning a musical instrument, get a good teacher –
it saves a lot of time

Practice is necessary for any skill, but it doesn't always 'make perfect'- you need to practise the right technique

18

If you see something you really love, buy it, even if it is expensive – you don't find things you love very often

Be in control of your body, rather than letting your body control you

20

When faced with a difficult task, make a start and it becomes easier. Don't over-think it

Accept who you are

22

Don't be too harsh on other people's faults

Always, always make sure all your car windows
are clear before driving off

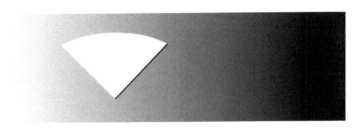

24

Pray – even though God sometimes doesn't answer it, he always hears it

Read the Bible

26

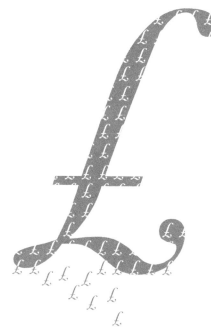

Have a budget, then only withdraw
that amount of cash for spending

If you find an item of clothing that looks really good on you, consider buying two of them

28

Don't shower every day

Gardening is a great thing to do, and it teaches you a lot

30

SING

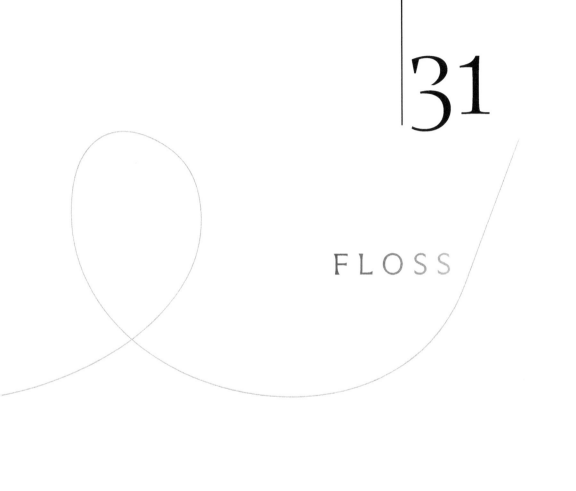

31

FLOSS

32

Do not go to bed late: early to bed, early to rise, really *does* make a man healthy, wealthy and wise

33

Never read with the telly on – you can't
read properly like that

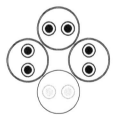

34

Go to church every Sunday without fail

35

Tell others about God

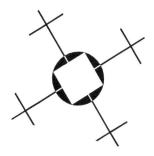

36

Be very selective about who you ask for advice

37

Nothing in this life will ever be perfect or complete

38

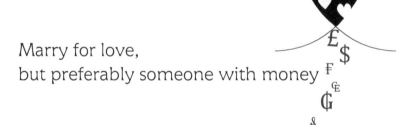

Marry for love,
but preferably someone with money

Writing things down will soon clarify something that seemed very muddled in your head

40

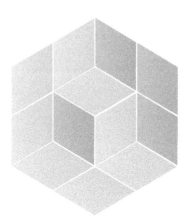

We often make the mistake of thinking that a thing has to be one thing or the other, when actually it is both

Don't do something nice to compensate for something bad.
Do something nice for the pleasure of it in itself.
E.g. if there has been a family row, don't go out for a nice
meal to make up for it

42

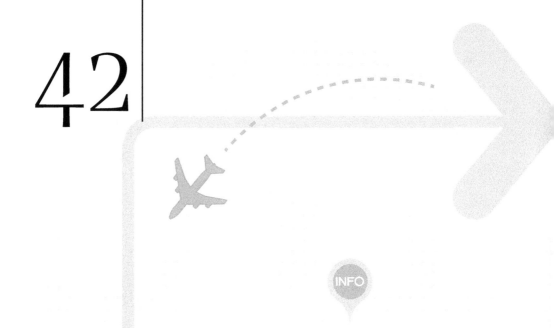

When on holiday go first to the local tourist information; get a good map of the area and a list of the top attractions

43

Honey and lemon drinks will not cure a cold, but they will make you feel a bit better.

This is an important lesson in life: do the little things that will make your situation better. Do not neglect the little things just because they won't make the problem completely disappear – they are still worth doing[1]

44

When out on the town, insert one or two soft drink 'spacers' between alcoholic drinks. This will interrupt the flow of alcohol consumption which is very effective in preventing excess.

You will be glad you did this after the event

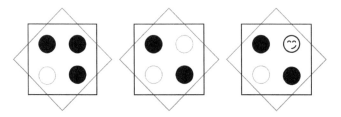

45

Drink Pepsi or Coca Cola when you are feeling
a bit rough – it makes you feel better

46

It is an amazing fact of life that sometimes a tiny
adjustment can make a huge difference.
It is very easy to overlook this fact

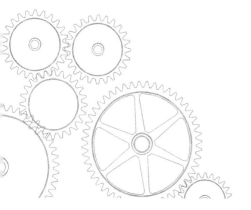

47

Some of the best things in life are indeed free, for example walking in beautiful countryside, a beach, good conversation, music, love

48

Your lifestyle must match your income

49

It is much more humiliating for a woman to be rejected than for a man. Therefore men have to make the first move. Don't wait for a woman to make the first move, just go for it and laugh it off if you are rejected

50

If someone is laughing at your mistake, consider laughing with them. It can neutralise your embarrassment. The exception to this is if someone is going too far and attacking you (with words or physically) - then you must fight back

Stand UP to people who are out of order

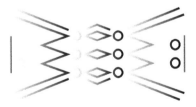

52

If you do not know what to say in a difficult
situation, say something like:
'I don't feel this is right' or
'I need time to think about this'.

Buy yourself time – do not commit to
anything or let people off the hook just
because you are under pressure

The closest we ever come to altruism is when we are responsible for someone on a one-to-one basis

54

Much of a man's social conscience is an overspill from his own emotional baggage

55

If you see someone in trouble, help them;
even if this means risking your own safety

56

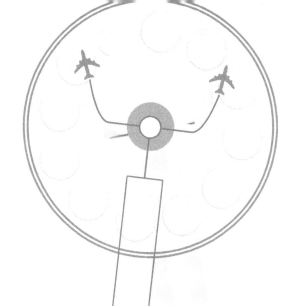

When planning an itinerary, always plan in some free time

If you have a garage, don't fill it with junk.
Put your car in it in the winter

58

If snow is forecast have a shovel and some grit handy

Allow plenty of time to tackle a DIY job
– avoid the temptation to take short cuts

60

Use the right tool for the job

When giving a speech or a talk, do not just read out a text to your audience — it never works. As hard as it may sound, you have to speak to your audience spontaneously so that your words are chosen in the moment. Written notes should just be a reminder of the themes you wish to cover

62

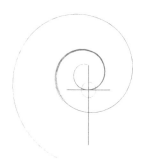

A good preacher speaks from his heart….to my heart….
about God's heart

Invest in decent waterproof clothing: boots, jacket, trousers

64

Staying indoors for too long is not healthy.
Go for a walk to blow away the cobwebs

65

Walking helps you think

66

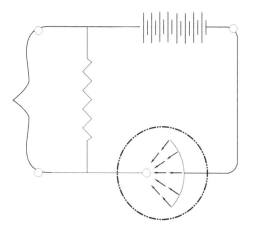

Don't watch too much telly – read instead

Some people seem to have more natural authority
than others

68

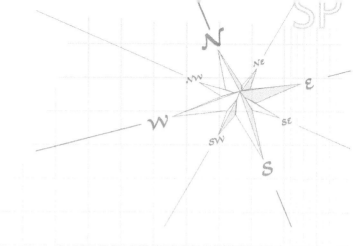

Learn how to use an ordinance survey map

A good meal out is one which leaves you with as much pleasure during and after it as in the anticipation of it

70

Don't try to re-live a numinous experience from the past. You can never go back. Just enjoy the memory[2]

Problems do not usually turn out to be as bad as you feared. Things have a way of working out

72

Don't get your kids to record your answer-machine message

73

During an important telephone call, when you are nervous and trying to impress, be aware of the tone of your voice and try to stop it going too high

74

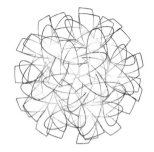

When having one of those conversations where both of you seem to be speaking at the same time, relax, slow down and let the other person speak

Listen to your children with your full and undivided attention. This is harder than it sounds, but very rewarding

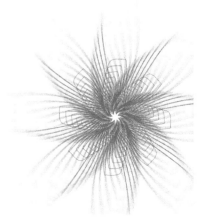

76

Always arrange display items in groups of odd numbers,

never even

Be honest with yourself when designing the décor and layout of a space – if something doesn't look very good don't settle for it

78

If the number of your possessions is greater than the
space you have to contain them……
you know what to do!

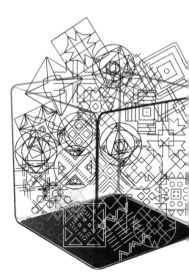

		8	3			2		
	6	4	8					
	2					8	7	
					7			
				1		5		
5	7		6					
6			4			3		
	7	5						9
9				8				

79

Trust yourself to remember numbers without having to go back and check them

80

It is assumed these days that brain states determine our behaviour and our experience. However, there is such a thing as free will and free will can never be accounted for by reference to brain states – if it could, it would not be free; it would be determined by biological antecedents. Free will and subjective experience (what it feels like to me to be me) stand outside of a physical explanation and are evidence of a mind/body dualism

We foolishly pathologize every behaviour that deviates from the norm. We bow to scientific materialism which squeezes free will out of the picture. We look to a diagnosis rather than human beings for an explanation. As this paradigm dominates we surrender crucial aspects of our humanity: personal responsibility, the uniqueness of the individual, the freedom to live how we want

82

The medical profession has allowed itself to be sharpened like a pencil – it now consists of a fine tip with which to execute highly technical procedures but the doctor-patient relationship has been shaved off and discarded

Men should be men and women should be women –
we have a given nature

People are only motivated to do anything for one of two reasons: to experience pleasure or to reduce anxiety. A life characterised by an excessive drive to reduce anxiety ends up closing down the possibilities for enjoyment. But....if we do not experience enough anxiety to be a 'good' person we will become an unproductive slob.

A balance is required!

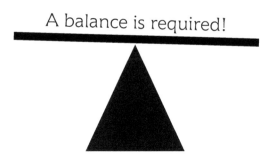

85

Happiness is always on the move; don't try to pin it

down

86

God didn't give us computer games or TVs. When we enjoy the natural world we are living according to our true nature and we will experience a deeper, more grounded sense of joy

Man is supremely adaptable –
this is a blessing and a curse

88

When cycling on the road always assume the
worst of other road users

Store
things
in boxes

not bags

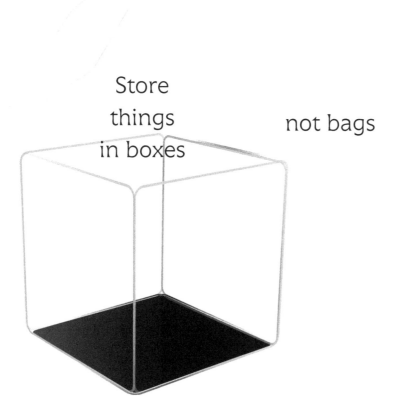

90

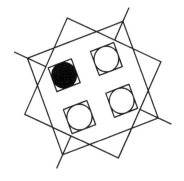

As a manager I work on the principle that if something can go wrong, it will

Don't expect your friends to do jobs for you for free

Never lend anything that you are not prepared to lose

When we are young we are faced with many situations that are not good and which we do not have the capacity to change. Our tendency is to employ psychic defences which have the effect of reconstructing the bad thing in our minds so that it no longer seems a bad thing. However, in reality it is still a bad thing. As we get older we must move away from such defensive mechanisms and instead try to change the real situation. If this remains beyond our power, we must accept it for what it really is and not attempt to 'change it in our minds'

94

Don't employ a cleaner – clean your own mess!

Don't employ a child minder – you can't substitute the love of a parent

96

Spend time with horses and dogs

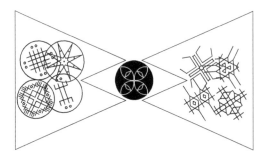

97

Be careful not to force your likes and dislikes onto
your children: let them find their own

98

Do not give children too much choice

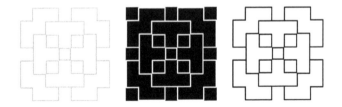

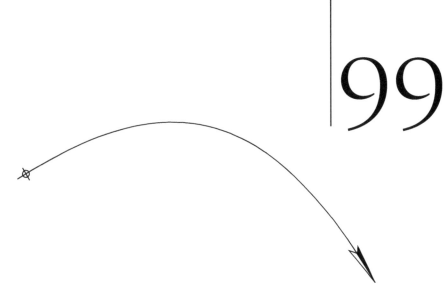

99

Avoid over-reaching – in all senses of the word

100

Keep gloves in your glove box

Often things can only be enjoyed or have benefit if taken in the correct measure[3]

102

There is a very fine line between a lovely cup of tea and an undrinkable one

If you want to be tough……you've got to **be** tough

104

To improve your swimming you have to sacrifice speed in order to concentrate on technique. This principle may apply to other walks of life

When finishing a conversation or a meeting it is not necessary to round it off with a neat summary. By all means do this if it comes naturally but otherwise a simple 'OK, see you' is fine

106

Don't live by a maxim without first considering if it is actually true or not

107

Say thank you to God when He has given you
what you asked for

108

"If you look good, you feel good and if you feel good maybe you will do good"[4]

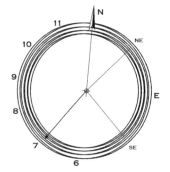

Choosing where to go on holiday throws up the dilemma of whether to seek excitement from something new or the pleasure of the familiar. In the former you waste time getting your bearings. In the latter you make better use of your time at the expense of the stimulation of new discoveries. Perhaps alternate!

110

Humility in a self confident person is extremely attractive.
I imagine Jesus had those qualities

Regarding musical composition:
"If it sounds good, it is good" [5]

112

In any creative endeavour you have to 'murder your darlings': in a piece of writing only include what is strictly necessary for that piece. Resist the temptation to shoe-horn anything in, no matter how cherished. The same applies to musical composition: only include what is right for the song

113

Life is for living

114

Anxieties are much more apparent at the start of something than towards the end

When I was young I didn't see earning
potential as a priority in my career choice.
Now that I am older I wish I had

116

If you want something badly enough you will get it

117

If you want to lose weight you have to stop thinking about losing weight and get on with the pain of actually eating less. You can't think yourself thinner

118

If people are genuinely interested in 'facts' they will have a discussion, not an argument. An argument is not really a dispute about facts, it is when two emotional positions are in conflict. A successful resolution to an argument can only be reached when these emotional positions are acknowledged and respected, regardless of the 'facts'

It is no use feeding the body when the soul is hungry

120

As a parent the trick is to know just when and just how much to interfere in your child's life

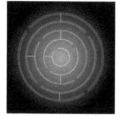

Sometimes we reach a dead end in our life where we realise we are unable to make everything right by our own efforts. At this point the first thing to do is stop trying. We must acknowledge we can't do it on our own and we must ask God to step in

The only difference between modern man and
Adam is that the technology has moved on a bit

Always try to fix something yourself before
parting with money

124

When going out on any sort of day trip,
take a backpack

Children need a bit of cajoling and persuading in order to widen their experience but don't be too much of a nag. They may turn into nags themselves and inflict it back on you

126

When someone says 'I absolutely love sushi' what they mean is that they love the fact that they can tolerate sushi because this means they can go around telling people they love sushi

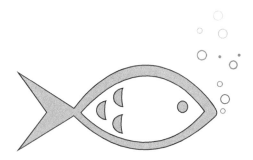

I can't help feeling suspicious of adults who
remain fussy eaters

128

Aftershave: apply sparingly, if at all

"Iron sharpeneth iron; so a man sharpeneth the countenance of his friend" [6]

130

Don't expect children to enjoy adult things, like going for walks or looking at a view. Just as the level of energy, light and mood changes in the course of one day, so it is that in the 'morning' stage of life we are naturally inclined to do different things than in the 'afternoon' phase, and vice versa[7]

We are more ready to blame others when secretly
we know we are at fault

132

A highly educated and intelligent person can use their rhetorical skills to persuade you that something is plausible when it is actually false. Judge an argument on its logical and factual merits and not on the apparent credentials of the speaker

If someone has the audacity to try to rip you off, the least you can do is have the audacity to challenge them

134

Pushing a child before he's ready is like picking a blackberry before it's ripe

We all end up worshipping something. It may as
well be Jesus Christ

136

When someone comes to your home or your office
greet them by saying: 'Welcome'

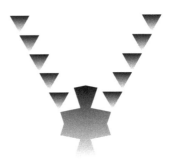

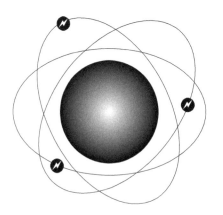

137

In the final analysis, power can only be guaranteed by
the possession of superior physical force

138

People are like sponges. Stuff comes out of them when they are squeezed. Let it be the Holy Spirit![8]

Understand that there will be a discrepancy between
your 'ideal' child and your actual child

140

When playing a musical instrument, listen out for the bits in your playing that are not quite right. Don't settle for them! Don't gloss over them! Keep working on them until you get it right. This applies to all forms of playing - technique, composition, improvisation and transcribing

You can't make an omelette without breaking eggs. In order to create excitement in your life, or to stop yourself getting stuck in a rut, sometimes you have to take a bit of a risk and try something that may create waves

142

No good deed goes unpunished

If you've made a commitment don't cancel it
unless really necessary

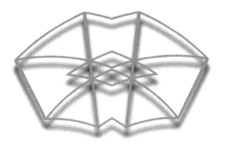

As a person develops he will construct a self-image which conforms to the 'conditions of worth' laid down by authority figures. This self-image will to some extent deviate from the 'true self', the latter being something like the pristine core of being that would develop according to its blue-printed nature, given permission and nurturing. The false self-image is 'happy' insofar as it is supplied with experiences that it thinks it should have. This is false happiness for a false self. The stronger the false self-image (the earlier it is laid down and the intensity of the pressure to conform to it), the 'happier' these individuals claim and appear to be. This is because they are so far away from the true self that it is not on their radar and they are less troubled by the dissonance. Conversely, the narrower the gap between the true and the false self, the more acute the depression - because the true self is sufficiently developed to perceive the loss. This type of depression consists in the level of awareness of the dissonance between the desires of the true self and the life that the self-image has insisted upon

......A 'successful' life is often the triumph of a
false self-image

146

Don't look upon housework as a chore; think of it as part of the natural rhythm of life

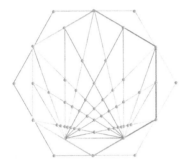

What is the essence of humanity? It is the convergence
of the animal nature and the divine nature;
and it is the interplay between them

148

Record your creative ideas when they arise, before you forget them

If you are in conflict with someone: whatever they do, go one further

What is love? I believe it is the feeling which arises when something other than you becomes partially incorporated in you. Love has the paradoxical quality of feeling both ephemeral, ungraspable, and yet painfully real. This is because love emerges at the point where oneself as a distinct entity interfaces with a state of being merged with an Other. You can only love that which is both you and not you

Allow your unconscious to guide you when you
are not sure what to do

152

Choose beauty over convenience

Just because we experience despair, it does not mean that all hope is lost. Just because we experience meaninglessness, it does not mean that there is no purpose to life. Yes, we have to accept the truth about how awful life can be sometimes, but we also have to take responsibility for making it better

154

'Stress' is an internal matter [9]

Desperation stinks

156

Careful preparation repays the required time and effort

157

Have respect for the way things have always been
done in the past

158

People do what they want to do

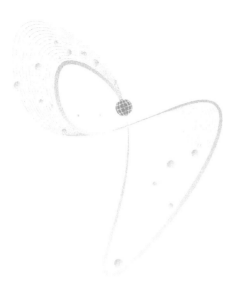

The world's psyche operates according to the same principles as the individual psyche. What we are seeing today is the start of a dispensation where the 'abject' (the world's poor) demands integration with the ego (the West). The response of the West to the inevitable flow of migration will often be defensive, arising from a fear that the unconscious will flood the ego; a fear of chaos and madness

160

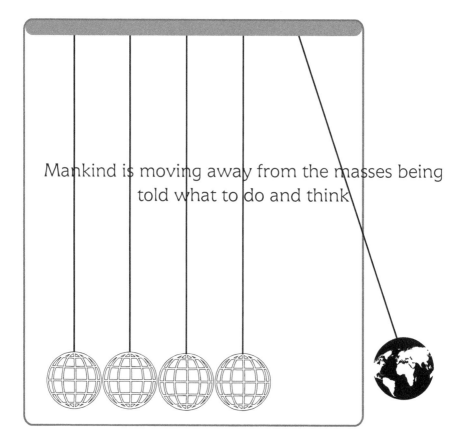

Mankind is moving away from the masses being told what to do and think

An act of true sacrificial love is like a diamond
on a pebble beach[10]

162

If you wait for perfection you end up with nothing

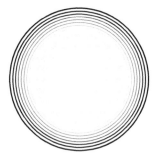

As a parent, try to metabolize your child's
anxieties, not project yours onto them

If you can't decide where to place something, e.g. where to pitch a tent or place an item of furniture: first identify where it can't go. This should narrow down the possibilities considerably, making the final decision much easier

When removing something from its packaging, take time to see how it's designed to be opened, rather than just ripping it open. Have a pair of scissors handy

166

If you start a task and you realise you are doing it wrong, start again. Don't try to save time by pressing on with the wrong way - this will take even more time

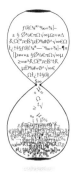

The start of a dog walk is full of excitation

168

If you ask someone a reasonable question but they do not bother to reply, assume the answer that is favourable to you

Similarly, when completing a badly worded form and there is ambiguity, assume the interpretation that is favourable to you, as long as this is reasonable

When you have not spent enough quality time with the precious things in your life - those things that are necessary for your soul - bitter regret builds up under the surface of your consciousness…and later gets acted out in dysfunctional ways. Hoarding is an example: it is the unconscious displacement of the regret of a wasted life. Regrets are inevitable, but do not let regrets accumulate in this way, instead acknowledge and 'discharge' them as you go along

The beauty of a garden consists in the wildness and endless variety of nature being harnessed and trained into a conscious design. Its enduring appeal is that this is a metaphor for the psychodynamic structure of the mind. For example, consider the primary importance of borders in a garden

Transfer food items into attractive bowls if they are
going to be stored anywhere on display

Never trust a salesperson. Never allow anything personal or emotional into the discussion - this is a technique to trap you. Sales discussions should always be cold

174

A woman leaving you can be very hard to accept. This is because it taps into the primitive, unthinkable terror of Mother leaving

175

We must learn to accept disappointment
when our efforts fail

176

Moaning about the annoying things in life is only satisfying for the person doing the moaning

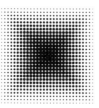

Don't give someone too many compliments

We should aim to balance the relationship between our primitive instinctual desires (the id) and our civilized, conscious mind (the ego). The id will return in some form anyway, so needs to be given expression, but it must be tempered and contained by the ego

It's worth spending money on something that is going to make your life a lot easier

180

A table is not for putting things on

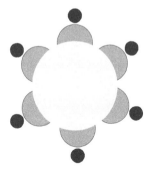

There are only two explanations: the absurdity of God, or the absurdity of a universe with no God. Choose your absurdity

182

When we test out our theories and inner thought processes in the outer world - by writing them down - we can get results that we didn't see or expect to begin with

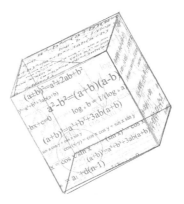

Learn to spot the occasions when it is wise to keep silent

Take the time to carry out basic car maintenance

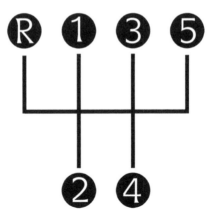

185

The proposition that the universe came from nothing
does not make sense to me

186

'Copy and paste' is causing us to be de-skilled in the
construction of logical sentences

Never assume you know best because you are more educated. You still have to think things through

188

Your employer is not your parent

The Mind-Body problem is the central issue for mankind

190

Sometimes you meet someone and there is a natural chemistry; conversation and laughter flow effortlessly. Sometimes not! That's just how it is

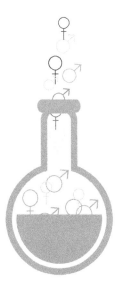

Read a dictionary for fun

192

Alcohol is a dangerous drug because it is so socially acceptable

Take photographs now and then. Install them as your screen saver, on a random shuffle

194

Keep a diary of some kind

Don't commit to something that you don't actually
want, or need, to do; learn to say 'no'

196

our first choice is usually right

Don't be one of those people who constantly under-estimate how long, expensive or difficult an undertaking will be

198

I've learnt to recognize at an early stage the stirrings of anxiety that arise when external pressures are building up. I can then take action to reduce those pressures before they become overwhelming

Work is work; it's part of life. It's no bad thing

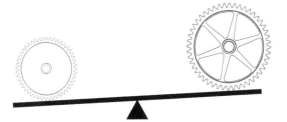

200

In a disagreement, be open to the possibility that you might be wrong and, if you are, admit it and apologize if necessary

If you keep getting into the same sort of relational problem with people, it's you, not everyone else, that is the likely cause

202

In order to clean something properly it is
necessary to apply ~~pressure~~

Learn how to do small talk; although it might seem trivial and contrived, the fact is that it's a necessary stepping stone to an interesting conversation and – who knows – maybe a friend for life![11]

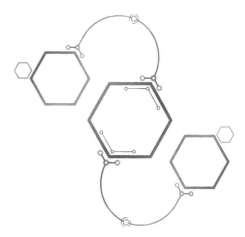

204

In boxing you have to be relaxed, yet very focused.
The same is true when playing a guitar solo – you
have to put the energy in when required to make
an impact, to get the impressive result....but...
you also have to relax, to have fluidity, in order to
create the space for the attack to come.

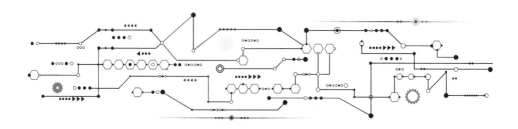

Don't think that just because you've read all this
good advice you now know everything!

$$\emptyset = \{\,\}$$

References:

[1] Adapted from an idea by James Richard O'Neill

[2] Adapted from an idea by Darren Nathaniel O'Neill

[3] Inspired by the 'Honorary Consul' by Graham Greene

[4] Jason O'Neill

[5] Yngwie J Malmsteen

[6] Proverbs 27:17 (King James Version)

[7] Based on Carl Gustav Jung

[8] Based on a sermon by Rev David Lewis

[9] Dr Jonathan Holbrook

[10] See Luke 21 1:4

[11] Adapted from an idea by Rachel O'Neill

Mark O'Neill

Mark O'Neill is 47, married with two children and lives in Surrey. He studied Philosophy at the University of Sussex and ended up as a manager in the health sector. In later years he trained in psychotherapy at the University of Roehampton and currently has a small private practice as a psychodynamic counsellor. In his spare time he enjoys writing, playing guitar, and walking the countryside.

Index

(Thematic in bold)

Lightning Source UK Ltd.
Milton Keynes UK
UKHW05f0533210218
318246UK00003B/7/P